PITTSBURGH PIRATES

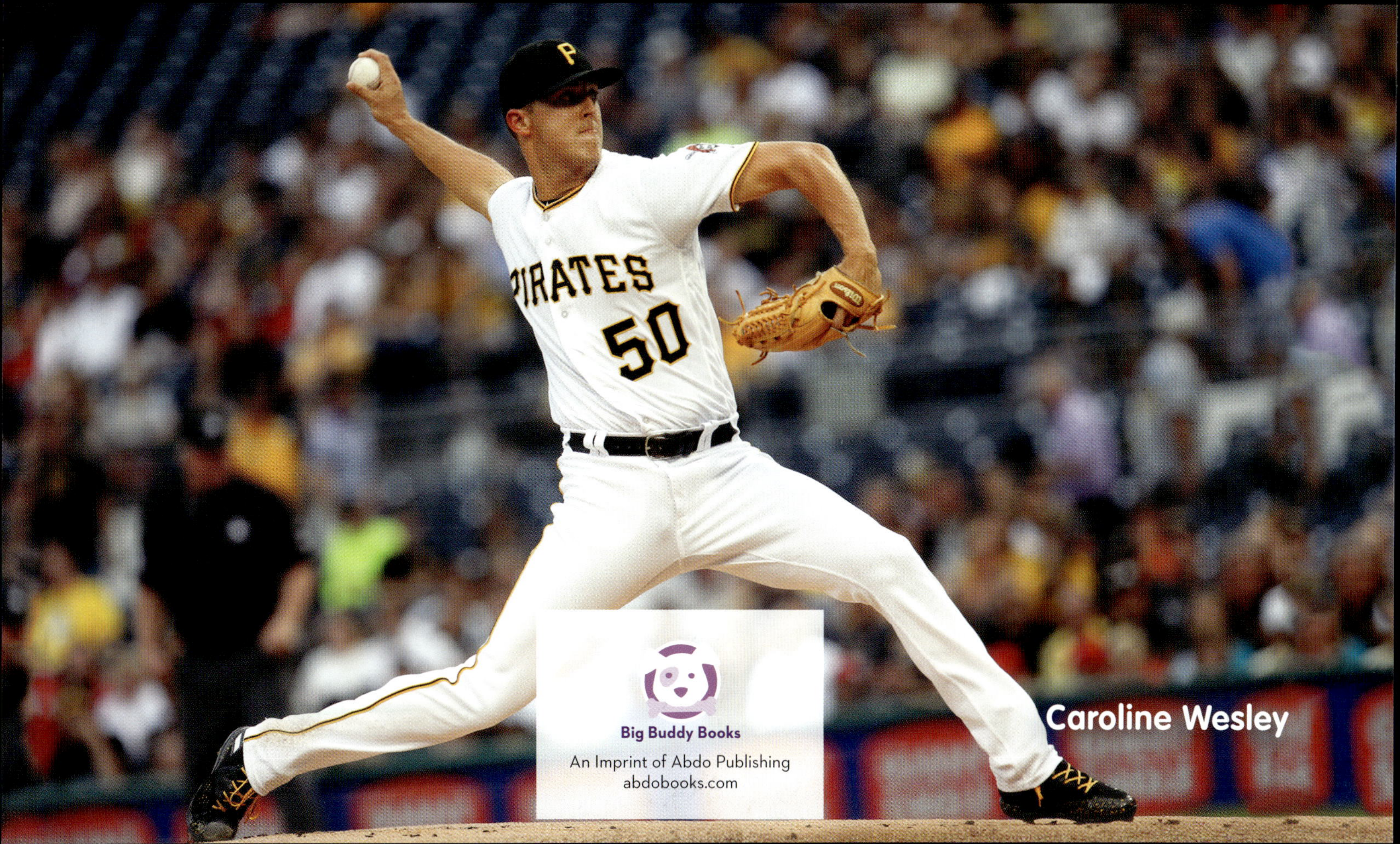

Caroline Wesley

Big Buddy Books
An Imprint of Abdo Publishing
abdobooks.com

abdobooks.com

Published by Abdo Publishing, a division of ABDO, PO Box 398166, Minneapolis, Minnesota 55439.

Printed in the United States of America, North Mankato, Minnesota.
102018
012019

Cover Photo: Justin K. Aller/Getty Images.
Interior Photos: 33ft/Depositphotos (p. 7); AP Images (pp. 11, 19, 22, 28); Brian Blanco/Getty Images (p. 24); Chris Hondros/Getty Images (pp. 22, 29); Doug Mills/AP Images (p. 23); Elsa/Getty Images (p. 25); Everett Collection Inc/Alamy Stock Photo (p. 13); Ezra Shaw/Getty Images (p. 17); J. Meric/Getty Images (pp. 24, 25); Joe Sargent/Getty Images (pp. 5, 27); Keith Srakocic/AP Images (pp. 9, 15); Lennox McLendon/AP Images (p. 21); Patrick Smith/Getty Images (p. 29); PS/AP Images (p. 23).

Coordinating Series Editor: Tamara L. Britton
Contributing Editor: Jill M. Roesler
Graphic Design: Jenny Christensen, Cody Laberda

Library of Congress Control Number: 2018948452

Publisher's Cataloging-in-Publication Data

Names: Wesley, Caroline, author.
Title: Pittsburgh Pirates / by Caroline Wesley.
Description: Minneapolis, Minnesota : Abdo Publishing, 2019 | Series: MLB's greatest teams set 2 | Includes online resources and index.
Identifiers: ISBN 9781532118135 (lib. bdg.) | ISBN 9781532171178 (ebook)
Subjects: LCSH: Pittsburgh Pirates (Baseball team)--Juvenile literature. | Baseball teams--United States--History--Juvenile literature. | Major League Baseball (Organization)--Juvenile literature. | Baseball--Juvenile literature.
Classification: DDC 796.35764--dc23

Contents

Major League Baseball

League Play

There are two leagues in MLB. They are the American League (AL) and the National League (NL). Each league has 15 teams and is split into three divisions. They are east, central, and west.

The Pittsburgh Pirates is one of 30 Major League Baseball (MLB) teams. The team plays in the National League Central **Division**.

Throughout the season, all MLB teams play 162 games. The season begins in April and can continue until November.

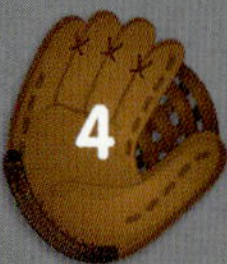

The Pirate Parrot mascot joined the Pirates in 1979. He helped create the "Let's Go Bucs, Let's Go Green" campaign. This movement helps save the planet!

A Winning Team

The Pirates team is from Pittsburgh, Pennsylvania. The team's colors are black, gold, and white.

The team has had good seasons and bad. But time and again, players have proven themselves. Let's see what makes the Pirates one of MLB's greatest teams!

Fast Facts

HOME FIELD: PNC Park

TEAM COLORS: Black, gold, and white

TEAM SONG: "A New Pirates Generation" by Buzz Poets

PENNANTS: 9

WORLD SERIES TITLES: 1909, 1925, 1960, 1971, 1979

CANADA
UNITED STATES OF AMERICA
MEXICO
N
W
E
S
LAKE ERIE
New York
Ohio
Pennsylvania
Pittsburgh
New Jersey
West Virginia
Maryland
ATLANTIC OCEAN

PNC Park

The Pirates have been in Pittsburgh since 1887. The team has played in five different stadiums throughout the city. The Pirates played at Recreation Park as the Alleghenys until 1890. Then it moved to Exposition Park, Forbes Field, and Three Rivers Stadium.

The team played at Three Rivers Stadium for 30 years. Finally in 2001, it settled at PNC Park in downtown Pittsburgh. The ballpark sits along the shore of the Allegheny River.

Pittsburgh is also home to professional football and hockey teams the Steelers and the Penguins. Like the Pirates, the Steelers' and Penguins' team colors are black, gold, and white.

Then and Now

The Allegheny team began in 1882. Five years later, it joined the NL. In 1890, the team had the lowest record it would ever see. Players won only 23 out of 136 games. The owners knew they had to rebuild the roster.

The team added valuable players to its lineup. At the same time, the Alleghenys changed its name to the Pittsburgh Pirates. Over the next decade, the Pirates continued to advance in the league.

In 1903, the team played the Boston Americans in the first-ever World Series. Sadly, the Pirates lost five of the eight games.

After losing the 1903 World Series, the Pirates began posting winning seasons. In 1909, the Pirates made it to the World Series once more. The team won its first Series title against the Detroit Tigers.

The players had 11 winning seasons over the next 15 years. But they did not make it to the **playoffs** during that time. Then in 1925, players Pie Traynor and Kiki Cuyler led the team to the World Series. They won four games to three over the Washington Senators.

US President Calvin Coolidge threw the first pitch in Game Three of the 1925 World Series.

Highlights

During the 1930s and 1940s, the Pirates won more than half of the seasons played. But the players struggled during the 1950s. They finished in seventh or eighth place for eight straight seasons.

The losing streak ended when the team jumped to second place in 1958. Two years later, it was back in the **playoffs**.

The Pirates made it all the way to the 1960 World Series. There, they beat the New York Yankees four games to three!

In Game Seven of the 1960 World Series, the Pirates were last to bat. Bill Mazeroski hit the final pitch, and it was a home run! This had never happened in World Series history.

From 1970 to 1980, the Pirates made it to the **playoffs** six times. The players collected four **division** titles and two World Series titles.

In the 1980s, the team had five winning seasons. And they made it to the playoffs three more times from 1990 to 1993.

Over the next 20 years, players fought to place higher than third place in the division. Starting in 2013, the team made it to the playoffs three years straight.

Win or Go Home

The top team from each AL and NL division goes to the playoffs. Each league also sends one wild-card team. One team from the AL and one from the NL will win the pennant. The two pennant winners then go to the World Series!

There are 37 past Pirates players in the National Baseball Hall of Fame. There are also nine past managers honored there.

Famous Managers

Danny Murtaugh was one of the most successful Pirates managers. He managed on and off for 19 years. During the 1970s, Murtaugh helped the Pirates make it to the **playoffs** five times. And he led the players to two World Series victories!

Throughout his **career**, Murtaugh won six Manager of the Year Awards. In 1977, the Pirates **retired** Murtaugh's jersey number 40 in his honor.

Murtaugh *(right)* retired as manager of the Pirates four times during the 1960s and 1970s!

Chuck Tanner managed the Pirates from 1977 to 1985. His first year, he led the team to 96 wins. Two years later, he helped the team to a World Series victory!

After 1979, the Pirates had four more winning years under Tanner's leadership. Later, he was **nominated** for the 1983 NL Manager of the Year Award. Tanner went on to manage the Atlanta Braves in 1986.

Tanner *(center)* managed the winning 1980 NL All-Star team.

Star Players

1900 – 1917

Honus Wagner SHORTSTOP, #33

Honus Wagner is one of history's greatest ball players. In 1902 and 1906, Wagner led the league in number of runs scored. He even won eight batting titles for his skills at the plate. Wagner led the Pirates to its first World Series win in 1909. He joined the National Baseball Hall of Fame in 1936.

Roberto Clemente RIGHTFIELDER, #21

Roberto Clemente was an all-star batter and outfielder. In 1961, he won his first NL batting title for his powerful swing. He also earned a **Gold Glove** for fielding. Clemente won three more batting titles and 11 more Gold Glove Awards. And in 1971, he earned the World Series **Most Valuable Player (MVP)** Award.

1955 – 1972

Willie Stargell LEFTFIELDER, #8

Willie Stargell was one of the best Pirates players for 21 seasons. He won the **Championship** Series, World Series, and regular-season **MVP** awards in 1979. He was the first player to do so. During his **career**, he helped the Pirates win six **division** titles and two World Series.

Barry Bonds LEFTFIELDER, #24

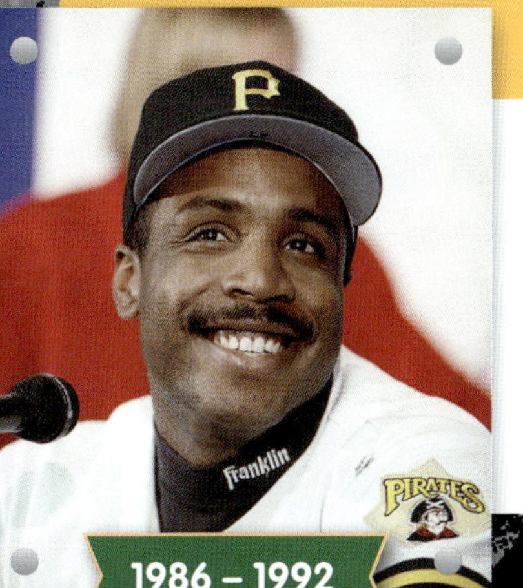

World-famous slugger Barry Bonds began his MLB career with the Pirates. In only seven years with the team, he hit 176 home runs! Bonds earned three **Silver Sluggers** for his efforts. He also won the 1990 Major League Player of the Year Award.

Starling Marte OUTFIELDER, #6

Starling Marte grew up in the Dominican Republic. He joined the Pirates when he was 23 years old. As an outfielder, Marte has **putout** more than 1,000 batters! For his fielding skills, he won the 2015 Wilson Defensive Player of the Year Award. He also earned **Gold Glove Awards** in 2015 and in 2016.

Gregory Polanco OUTFIELDER, #25

Gregory Polanco plays as an outfielder for the Pirates. In five years with the team, he has putout nearly 900 batters! As a batter himself, Polanco has scored more than 250 runs for his team. In 2017, he played in the World Baseball Classic for Team Dominican Republic.

Jordy Mercer SHORTSTOP, #10

Jordy Mercer began his MLB **career** as the Pirates' shortstop and second baseman. Mercer has **putout** more than 800 batters as shortstop. He has also fielded nearly 2,000 **assists**. In 2017, Mercer hit 14 home runs. That same year, he played in 1,241 **innings**.

Josh Bell FIRST BASEMAN, #5

Josh Bell was **drafted** in 2011 once he finished high school. After his first season, Bell placed third in the NL **Rookie** of the Year voting. In 2017, he hit 26 home runs. That means that Bell broke the NL record for most homers by a rookie **switch-hitter**!

Final Call

All-Stars

The best players from both leagues come together each year for the All-Star Game. This game does not count toward the regular season records. It is simply to celebrate the best players in MLB.

The Pirates have a long, rich history. The team has played in seven World Series, and earned five World Series titles.

Even during losing seasons, true fans have stuck by the players. Many believe the Pirates will remain one of the greatest teams in MLB.

In 2018, pitcher Jameson Taillon *(left)* pitched a shutout game against the Cincinnati Reds. That means the Reds did not score any points in that game.

Through the Years

1887

The team played its first NL game in front of nearly 10,000 fans.

1900

Barney Dreyfuss took over as owner of the Pirates. He brought future Hall of Fame winners Honus Wagner and Fred Clarke with him.

1921

The Pittsburgh KDKA radio station played an MLB game on the radio for the first time. In that game, the Pirates beat the Philadelphia Phillies eight to five.

1937

Pirates' first baseman Gus Suhr played his eight hundred eighty-second game in a row.

1972

Roberto Clemente died in an airplane crash. He was delivering supplies after an earthquake in Central America.

2000

More than 55,000 fans attended a game at Three Rivers Stadium. It was the largest crowd to ever attend a regular-season Pirates game.

2016

The 1909 to 1911 Honus Wagner baseball card sold for $3.12 million. The Wagner card is the most valuable of all baseball cards.

2017

The Pirates took part in the very first MLB Little League Classic.

Glossary

assist the action of a player who by passing a ball makes it possible for a teammate to make a putout.

career a period of time spent in a certain job.

championship a game, a match, or a race held to find a first-place winner.

division a number of teams grouped together in a sport for competitive purposes.

draft a system for professional sports teams to choose new players.

Gold Glove Award annually given to the MLB players with the best fielding experience.

inning a division of a baseball game that consists of a turn at bat for each team.

Most Valuable Player (MVP) the player who contributes the most to his or her team's success.

nominate to name as a possible winner.

playoffs a game or series of games to determine a championship or break a tie.

putout an action that causes a batter or runner on the opposite team to be out.

retire to give up one's job, or to withdraw from use or service.

rookie a player who is new to the major leagues until he meets certain criteria.

roster an orderly list of people belonging to a professional sports group.

Silver Slugger Award given every year to the best offensive players in MLB.

switch-hitter a batter who can bat on either side of the plate.

Online Resources

To learn more about the Pittsburgh Pirates, visit **abdobooklinks.com**. These links are routinely monitored and updated to provide the most current information available.

Index